The Adventures of Salt and Soap at Grand Canyon

by Lori April Rome

Illustrations by Tanja Bauerle

GRAND CANYON ASSOCIATION

Grand Canyon Association
P.O. Box 399
Grand Canyon, AZ 86023-0399
(800) 858-2808
www.grandcanyon.org

Manufactured in China by C&C Offset Printing Co. Ltd. Shenzhen, Guangdong Province, in June 2010, Job #HK2100

Edited by Todd R. Berger

Designed by Ron Short

Back cover photograph by Todd R. Berger, Copyright © 2009 by the Grand Canyon Association

First Edition

13   12   11   10   3   4   5

Library of Congress Cataloging-in-Publication Data

Rome, Lori April, 1971-

  The adventures of Salt and Soap at Grand Canyon / by Lori April Rome ; illustrations by Tanja Bauerle. -- 1st ed.

    p. cm.

  ISBN 978-1-934656-04-4 (alk. paper)

  1. Mutts (Dogs)--Arizona--Grand Canyon--Anecdotes--Juvenile literature. 2. Grand Canyon (Ariz.)--Anecdotes--Juvenile literature. I. Bauerle, Tanja, 1970- ill. II. Title.

  SF426.5.R63 2009

  636.709791'32--dc22

                    2008034364

It is the mission of the Grand Canyon Association to cultivate knowledge, discovery, and stewardship for the benefit of Grand Canyon National Park and its visitors.

Proceeds from the sale of this book will be used to support the educational goals of Grand Canyon National Park.

Author's Dedication

This book is dedicated to mixed-breed dogs everywhere and the people who love them.

Illustrator's Dedication

For Kevin, Isabelle, and Zoe. You are the sunshine in my life. And to Otto and Peanut for their inspiration and companionship.

Author's Acknowledgments

I would like to thank everyone who has offered care for and support of Salt and Soap during their adventures in the Grand Canyon and throughout their lives. I would also like to thank the Grand Canyon Association and Tanja Bauerle for bringing this story to life; Grand Canyon National Park for providing inspiration and a home; the National Park Service for protecting special places; my husband, Kevin, for making a family with me and the pups; and Salt and Soap, who remind me everyday what is most important in life: love.

Illustrator's Acknowledgments

Thank you to my family, my parents, and all the friends in my mums' group, whose unfailing support has allowed me

to pursue my love for illustration.

Under a brilliant blue sky, two puppies lay napping side by side. Paws wiggle and whiskers twitch as dreams of adventure fill their sleepy heads. Red earth carpets the ground of this warm Arizona wilderness on the eastern rim of the Grand Canyon. There is little shade. Ravens soar overhead. A cottontail hides in the brush, while a coyote waits patiently to make chase.

The scent of sagebrush catches the wind, and a distant noise awakens the pups. Curious, they jump up to investigate. Voices fill the dry air. Soon, the pups see National Park Service rangers hiking toward them. The pups run to greet them. Surprised to see puppies in such a remote area of the park, the rangers bend down to scratch the little dogs' ears. The pups roll over and wiggle with excitement as the rangers rub their bellies.

Park rangers help care for special places like Grand Canyon National Park. These rangers have come for a patrol hike into the Grand Canyon to meet Colorado River rangers at the bottom. The pups peer over the rim to watch as their new friends descend the trail. The pups follow. They have never ventured into the canyon. Parks are for wild animals, not puppies, but the pups don't know that. They jump over huge boulders and bound down steep slopes. They dash sure-footedly around cactuses and keep a step ahead of the rangers. They all hike deeper and deeper into the Grand Canyon.

It is sunset when the rangers and pups reach the Colorado River. At the river, the red, pink, and orange rock walls are very tall, and the pups feel small as bugs. They greet the river rangers with yips and licks. All these new friends! The rangers marvel at how strong and brave the pups are for being so little, yet hiking so far. The rangers name the white pup Salt, for the dry creek bed they hiked down, and the black-and-brown one Soap, after a nearby side canyon. The pups squeal in delight. After dinner, Salt and Soap curl up on a ranger's raft and quickly fall asleep.

Plip…plop…plip…plop, plip, plop! It starts to rain. Boom!

Thunder shakes the pups' raft and lightning streaks above! The thunder scares the pups.

They jump off the boat, dash into a tent, and snuggle up next to a ranger.

The warmth of their bodies relaxes both the ranger and the pups.

Thank goodness for friends in hard times!

The next morning, the river rangers continue their trip. Salt and Soap want to go, but the rangers hiking out of the canyon lure the pups with treats. The pups follow the rangers as they head back up the trail. At the rim, the rangers see homes in the distance. The rangers tell the pups to go home, far from the dangers of the canyon and the river. But the pups peer down the trail at the river far below. After the rangers are gone, they head back into the canyon.

A dozen miles upriver, a group of friends launch their rafts for a two-week journey through the Grand Canyon. They are looking forward to the adventure of a lifetime! The river runners see many amazing things on their journey. Bighorn sheep drink along the riverbanks. Scavenging California condors circle overhead, searching for meals. At night, six-eyed scorpions wait on warm rocks to catch insects. But on this trip, the river runners see something even more amazing. Puppies! What on earth are puppies doing at the bottom of the Grand Canyon?

The river runners offer the dogs food, water, and attention. Later, as they sit around the campfire, the river runners discuss what to do. It is too hot to leave the puppies. Taking them on the river trip could be dangerous. What can be done? The group decides to take the pups with them downriver. They will carry them on the raft eighty miles to the ranger station at Phantom Ranch.

Splash! Swoosh! Slam!

Crashing rapids soon greet the river runners and the pups.

One rapid is especially fierce. Just after the raft enters the rapid—pow!

A huge wave hits, and the raft flips. Pups and people tumble into the icy-cold water.

The water pulls them under, then spits them back out. It is hard to breathe. Both the pups
and the river runners struggle to swim to shore. They all make it! Blankets, towels, and hot
drinks make the river runners and the pups feel better. They settle in for the night. Soon they
will reach Phantom Ranch.

A few days later at Phantom Ranch, the morning begins like any other. The Phantom Ranch rangers hike, watch for wildlife, and talk to hikers about nature. A "knock, knock, knock" is heard on the Phantom Ranch Ranger Station door. Ranger Lori opens the door and finds quite a surprise. Smiling river runners carry in two puppies and set them down on the floor. The pups sniff around this new place. After hearing the story of how the two pups got to the bottom of the Grand Canyon, Ranger Lori takes the puppies in as lost and found items. The pups bark and yip their goodbyes as the river runners head back to their rafts.

Now what? How will the puppies get out of the canyon? The nine-mile-long trail to the South Rim rises a mile in elevation. For now, the pups will stay with the rangers. Adorned with blue bandanas, rope leashes, and Junior Ranger badges, the pups help Ranger Lori check backpacking permits and make sure food is secured from wildlife at the campground. The pups befriend the campers. For now, they can help the rangers. Soon they will need to get back to a world with doghouses, water dishes, and plenty of kibble.

Whoosh, whoosh, whoosh, whoosh! A helicopter zooms into view and lands in the narrow canyon near Phantom Ranch. Everyone gives a belly rub to the pups. Where are they going to sit? Luckily, the crewmembers bring a doggie kennel. They place helmets on the pups' heads and let them sniff the inside of the helicopter. The pups then climb into the kennel. The helicopter blades start to turn again, and soon the puppies rise from the canyon floor. Hang on!

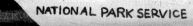

Canyon walls drop away as the helicopter rises higher into the sky.
The river soon looks like a watery thread. Birds fly far below. Puffy, white clouds appear
on the horizon. Whoosh, whoosh, whoosh, whoosh! The trip takes only eight minutes
before the helicopter gently touches down at the South Rim.

In the South Rim forest, Salt and Soap find a new home. They now live on the edge of the Grand Canyon with Ranger Lori. They stay in a house with a big yard. Elk and deer pass near their yard, and squirrels eat pinecones in the tree branches above as jays squawk. The pups nap in the summer sun and hide when thunderstorms boom overhead. Their paws and ears twitch nightly as they relive their journey. Never apart for a day in their lives, Salt and Soap sleep side by side, safe and loved, in their home at the Grand Canyon.

"Salt and Soap would like to thank all their friends at Grand Canyon
for offering love, friendship and the adventure of a lifetime."